inner voice

renuka i

LIFE
Inspiration and Personal Growth

This book contains original thoughts inspired by true life events of the author. Any resemblance is purely coincidental.

inner voice

A bbigg Book / published by bbigg Applications Inc.

PRINTING HISTORY
First Publication, eBook edition: April, 2018

ISBN: 978-0-9917358-2-2

dedication

to anyone looking to make room for reflection and
improvement in their lives.

acknowledgements

to my mom and brother: when I told you I wanted to write, you didn't stop me. and I'll tell you why this is important: blocks created against dreams are part of the reason people don't follow theirs. I'm grateful to you both for keeping my path clear for me.

to my dad: thank you for passing on your love of words to me. for never letting me forget that it is art, and it is beautiful. if you were here, I know you'd be proud.

to my beautiful sister, Dushy. on the darkest days, you are my light. I look for you in every sunrise, and every star. you're my motivation. I am brave enough to pursue my calling because you taught me how.

to my family and friends: your undying belief and relentless support is the reason I can do this with such freedom. I don't know why I've never had to face criticism from those closest to me, but I'm aware of its rarity and I thank you for being on my side.

to our future - Ava, Brayden, Ibby, Siona, Zoeya: we owe it to you to make this world a good place for you, precious souls to grow up in. and it starts within us – by taking the responsibility to be better human beings through thinking better, and doing better.

inner voice

you

there comes a time in life

when you stop thinking

about what this world has to offer you,

and start thinking

about what you have to offer this world.

what do you want?

whatever it is, it matters.

if it didn't,

you wouldn't wake up to the thought of it,

walk around with it,

lie at night with it.

you owe it to yourself to do something about it.

there are terrible people in this world.
and then there are good people who,
at a moment in time,
gave in to poor judgment
and behaved terribly.
there is a difference.
you are likely the latter.
stop beating yourself up over it.

learn how to think like a good human being
before you start acting like one.
no point in making noble moves
if your intentions are far from it.

there are going to be moments
where you wished you had handled a situation better.
sometimes you'll choose wrong,
even when you know right exists.
but it's better to be living here
than in a world where you did everything right.
because here,
you can be humbled by your mistakes.

if you want people to know
that you're a beautiful person,
a kind person,
a generous person,
a loving person,
a selfless person –
allow them to see it for themselves.
character is meant to be perceived,
not preached about.

you took the high road today.

maybe no one noticed.

maybe it didn't make a difference.

you're wondering why you even bother.

people noticed.

it made a difference.

the fact that you bothered

is a true testament to who you are.

learning to be a calm person
doesn't mean you have to transform into a pushover.
it's about perfecting the art of knowing
when something deserves a reaction,
and when it isn't worth it.

no point to your outer beauty

if you're ugly on the inside.

makeover your soul.

do it.

take that leap of faith.

you'll be as happy

as you pictured you would be

before fear made you hesitate.

go on, do it.

don't think with ifs anymore.

think with whens.

WHEN I achieve my goals,

WHEN my dreams become reality.

eliminate the ifs,

and life is no longer filled with maybes –

it's filled with definitelys.

no one is asking you
to never be angry, sad, frustrated.
expecting this from you
is expecting you to be less human.
you should however,
spend as little time as possible
in these negative feelings.
don't dwell in it longer than you must.

trust God with the details of your life.

attempting to handle everything on your own

will only slow down your journey.

get out of your own way.

are you sticking to this choice

because it's what you want?

or because it's easier to stay here

than it is to change?

you woke up this morning.

not everyone did.

that's reason enough to be grateful today.

sometimes you have to follow your gut.

even if it goes against reason.

intuition doesn't care about logistics.

its job is to give you a glimpse of your fate.

take a chance on it.

when your mind wanders
to negative places,
to worst case scenarios,
to dark spaces -
do not believe it.

get to know your pain.

get to know the pain of others.

involve yourself in it

instead of staring at it

from a safe distance.

to feel is an asset.

if you're yearning,

it's a sign you're not leading

the life you were meant to.

that longing you feel -

that's destiny trying to wake you up.

we're not better than anyone else.

we're not entitled to feel this way

just because of the education we've received

or the way that we look

or our place in society.

we need to reel in our superiority complexes.

no matter how fancy life becomes,

make sure your heart remains

in its humble beginnings.

the moment you decide

you're entitled to be somewhere higher –

is the day arrogance is born.

you don't have to like
what everyone else likes.

every so often,

remember life's preciousness.

focus on the lulls,

where nothing spectacular is happening.

we're just living.

with the people we love.

breathing as they breathe.

how extraordinary this is.

keep your private life

out of the public eye.

people can't interfere

if they have nothing to work with.

there is beauty in a person
who does good
and never speaks about it.

work hard

to be good to others

instead of working hard

to look good to others.

answering for your mistakes

is between you and God –

not you, God and them.

judging people is not our job.

our parents aren't perfect.

they may have made mistakes.

but we should learn from them -

not use them as the excuse

for why we're making the same ones.

yes, you could've done better.
and that's something
you must live with.
but it's not something
you must punish yourself for,
for the rest of your life.

when you want change

and it isn't happening,

change yourself.

sitting there waiting

for the world to re-adjust for you

is the reason why nothing is happening.

a person who genuinely wants to be better

will work at growing

even when no one is there to see it.

a person pretending to be better

will go back to their old ways

when their audience leaves.

it's possible

for someone else to be beautiful

without it being a threat to you.

one of your greatest accomplishments

will be the day you choose

to be happy with who you are.

every part of you.

the day you give up a version of you

for the real you.

to hate being wrong

is a bad quality to have.

because acknowledging

when you're wrong,

and accepting

when someone else is right

humbles you.

humility makes you wiser.

always being right, doesn't.

there's something special

about someone who goes out of their way to be kind.

not those who say thank you

when a door is held open for them –

but those who hold the door open.

not those who return the favour –

but those who give you a reason to return it.

if you think you're being kind enough,

there's room to be kinder.

life was never intended to be a struggle.

it's meant to be an opportunity

for knowledge and growth.

but if our calm is never disrupted,

we miss out on a lot of learning.

the next time you must face difficulty,

remind yourself that this is why.

the great thing about becoming

the best version of yourself:

when people try to be critical of you –

they have absolutely nothing to work with.

the good you do
in some areas of your life
doesn't erase the bad.
being a good person
isn't a part time job,
it's a full-time commitment.

don't let the bumps in the road deter you.

don't allow those negative people

to discourage you.

the sweetest victories

come after the hardest battles.

if you're wondering why

your mind always wanders to the same place,

it's because it's not wandering at all.

it's purposefully guiding

the rest of your body

to the place it believes you'll be your happiest.

if good came with ease,

everyone would have it,

no one would cherish it.

what's good is sometimes laced with struggle and pain.

but when it comes packaged like this,

you will appreciate it in ways you never could

had it just been handed to you.

sometimes you don't get what you want.

not because it's out of reach.

but because you didn't ask.

you are kind.

you are compassionate.

and don't you dare apologize for it.

in this desensitized world,

these traits have become foreign.

don't extinguish them to fit in.

if it dies,

humanity dies with it.

bad events in life are inevitable.

bad thoughts don't have to be.

negative thinking only complements catastrophe.

keep your mind positive

no matter how dreary the circumstances become.

sometimes

situations don't have a downside.

sometimes

they're just good,

and nothing but good.

stop trying to find negativity

where it doesn't exist.

you expect them

to accept you for you.

and yet,

you have problems

with them being them.

you know who you are now.
so, the days of being a chameleon -
changing colours
to suit your new friends,
new colleagues,
new boyfriend
should be behind you.

you may have an empire now.

but once upon a time,

it was just a pile of dreams.

don't forget

the people who helped you

build it brick by brick.

it is night.

go to sleep.

deal with it in the morning.

problems are always less severe

in the light of a new day.

sometimes we settle in life
because what we have now
is better than what we had.
that still isn't a valid excuse.
you deserve good,
not just good enough.

adversity teaches you
as much as it hurts you.
remember,
its lessons can never be replicated
in moments when life is good.

don't commit to things
if you can't follow through.
if you say you're going to be somewhere,
be there.
if you say you're going to do something,
do it -
no matter how insignificant it may seem.
reliability is a major building block of character.

you were looking for a sign, right?

here it is.

whatever it is you're going through right now,

you will get through it.

make it so there are no other options.

nothing is going to stop you from thriving.

hardships are ladders, not walls.

do not create a backup.

do not make a safer alternative.

when you have only one plan,

you follow your dreams

the way you're meant to:

wholeheartedly.

if this sounds risky to you,

it's because it is.

but a life without risks

becomes a life full of what-ifs.

and nothing is worth that.

keep going.

you've come this far.

you're closer than you were yesterday.

if you give up now,

you miss out on the best part:

you deserve to see how it ends.

be kind to the people you love.

make yourself a safe place

for them to come home to.

some days,

it's the only time they get to feel

real warmth and security.

let us learn to be better givers.

offer from what you love,

not from what you have left over.

every deliberate minute you spend

working on yourself

is a productive use of your time.

even if nothing else in your life

is in order,

you are succeeding.

no, you didn't fail.
you took a chance
on something you were passionate about,
and it didn't work out.
you eliminated a what-if from your life.
what part of that sounds like failure to you?

you don't always

have to respond to your critics.

sometimes silence is classier

than back and forth banter.

fighting fire with fire

only adds fuels to it.

revenge is not the way

to handle your problems.

be the one to put out the flames,

not the one who intensifies them.

eating clean

but indulging in hatred.

how will we ever be healthy?

believe,

no matter how bleak

the situation may seem.

miracles have no boundaries.

some are born

in the most unlikely places.

already being a good person
doesn't exempt you

from becoming a better one.

sometimes you're going to feel

like you don't know what you're doing.

and you're allowed to admit that.

life is an ongoing lesson.

it's okay

that we don't have it all figured out.

we're always in a hurry.

God – He's always on time.

if it were up to us,

we would rush life -

rush the money we want,

the career we want,

the love we want.

if we leave it up to God,

we can trust that He will deliver it

at the right moment.

it's better to be too kind

than not kind enough.

we have plenty

of awful people in this world.

never be mistaken

for one of them.

we all know

that we're sleeping in a bed tonight.

that we never have to worry

about how we're going to eat.

these concerns don't exist for us.

when was the last time

you were grateful

for what we regularly take for granted?

we all trip and fall along the way.

the thing that separates

those who fulfill their dreams

from the rest

is that they get back up

as quickly as they fall.

their focus

is on how far they've walked

before the misstep,

and how much closer

they are now.

they don't dwell on the fall,

they don't mourn it repeatedly.

that's the difference.

we think our lives are hard.

until we encounter someone

who would give anything

to live through our difficulty.

because what we're dealing with

is relief in comparison.

the more successful we become,

the more entitled we feel

to the love, money,

and respect that we have.

but every day

we should be waking up

and earning that love

from our loved ones,

earning our money,

earning respect.

and then going to sleep,

waking up the next day,

and earning it all over again.

this mentality will keep us grounded.

it's not too late to do something.

maybe you didn't get it right the first time,

but you can make it right this time.

not all your mistakes have to remain mistakes.

we spend so much time

preparing for later

that we fail to enjoy the present.

how soon we forget

that now is what we had prepared for

once upon a time,

in hopes that we would savour it

when the moment arrived.

and yet here we are...

if you must fight your feelings,

it's a sign that you're pushing away

something that you want...

you can relax.

you can take a break.

this doesn't have to be a luxury.

the only thing stopping you

is the choice you've made

to not make it one of your priorities.

don't let a regret remain a regret

simply because pride didn't allow you

to rectify it.

sometimes we're offended.

not because people are being offensive.

but because they're speaking the ugly truth about us.

and we can't handle it.

being optimistic 24/7 is impossible.

we are built to feel the highs and the lows.

so, feel them.

complain, get mad, cry.

sometimes it's what we need.

every morning

when we look out at the world

through our windows,

we must never forget

that we're free.

and then

we must remember

everyone else on earth,

who would give anything

to look out their windows,

and see the same thing.

it's hard

to shut the door on something,

especially when you don't want to.

so, don't.

don't shut the door.

just don't stand by it night and day anymore,

monitoring what's coming and going.

leave it open, go outside, live.

your desire will show up at your doorstep

when it's time.

don't have positive people around you?

become the positive person.

be the source you turn to for happiness.

learn to rely on yourself

the way you rely on others.

we think being in denial is saving us.

if we don't admit it,

it doesn't have to be true.

but denial is hindering us.

it's preventing our minds

from thinking what it wants to think,

and our hearts

from feeling what it wants to feel.

why don't you

stop swimming against the current

and see where it leads you instead?

make mistakes,

acknowledge them,

learn from them.

being perfect

is the wrong goal to have.

because someone who thinks

they never need improvement

has no room to grow.

achievements involve struggle.

so, if you're struggling,

it isn't a sign that you should give up.

it's part of what's inching you

closer and closer to your goal.

trust the process.

hatred isn't innate.

we aren't born with it -

we're born into it.

hatred is taught,

it is learned.

it's our fault that it exists.

so, stopping it

should be our responsibility, too.

every time it creeps in,
doubt is veering you off the path
towards living your dreams.
stop allowing it to interrupt the journey.

waiting for the right moment to act

is better than

acting because you're tired of waiting.

may today be the day

you've been waiting for.

not everything about your life

needs to be broadcasted.

deep within life,
as we get older,
and wiser,
and more experienced,
there is a place,
where love is real,
and good is real,
and joy is real.
and everything else
no longer exists.

logic is important

because it helps us make sense of life.

but anyone who has ever had a dream

didn't follow it because logic told them to.

sometimes it's necessary

to think with our hearts.

nothing wrong with living a fancy life.

you earned the money,

do what you want with it.

the problem lies in the fact

that you can afford to live five fancy lives

and choose not to share four of them

with someone else.

if something feels right,

maybe it's because it is.

the reason we second guess it

is because our mind walks in

and attempts to rationalize everything.

listen to your feelings.

if you don't fight for what you want,

you're going to lose it.

if this isn't reason enough

to push aside your fears,

your pride -

then you don't deserve it.

if you're deciding

whether or not you should make a move —

make the move.

if your heart didn't want you to act,

it would've never asked your mind

to think up the thought.

whatever gives you peace,
whoever gives you peace –
go there,
stay there.

if you have everything you want,

and you're still not fulfilled -

you have the wrong wants in life.

there are people in this world

who would give anything

to have your version of a crappy day.

if you're going to demand

that people do better,

you should expect

the same of yourself.

there's a blessing

in each and every circumstance.

you just never knew

to look for it in the bad, too.

trying to be good people in a bad world

is going to be our most difficult struggle.

and deserves our hardest fight.

protect your dream.
don't let anyone come in
and slash it,
take it apart,
throw pieces away.
you knew what you were doing
when you put it together.

there's nothing wrong

with working on your appearance.

sometimes we're just so focused on it

that we forget

there's more to us

than our looks.

if you're spending all your time

worrying about their mistakes,

who's going to fix yours?

or did you forget

that you're not perfect either?

what if our worries were positive

instead of negative?

if, "what if I fail?"

became "what if I actually make it?"

and, "what if I lose everything?"

became "what if I become rich?"

or "what if he doesn't love me?"

became "what if he really loves me?"

we need to change the way we worry.

the things you own
are not your blessings.

the wonderful thing

about this stage of adulthood

is that you know what you love,

and who you love.

and you're not sorry

for choosing them over everything else.

our brain is the most incredible tool.

you have the power to convince it of anything.

so, convince it of good things.

you and them

are you happy
or just comfortable?

there's a difference.

and only one

is worth sticking around for.

sometimes people come into your life

to show you that you deserve

so much more than them.

never assume

that your love is implied.

people need to

hear it, see it, feel it.

otherwise they will

yearn for it, then resent it, then leave it.

you're not losing

your ability to be patient.

as you get older,

you're just more aware

of the fact that certain people

no longer need to be tolerated.

a problem that involves

the both of you

can't be solved by

just one of you.

talk to each other.

when you don't do anything

about someone

who is treating you poorly,

it allows them to think

that it's okay to continue.

when you behave badly,

it's your fault.

when I let it get to me,

it's my fault.

no one has the power

to affect your mood

unless you allow it.

if you want insightful advice,

pay attention to the people

you're seeking it from.

both the good

and the bad sources

will tell you things

that you may not like.

but only the good ones

have your best interest at heart.

people get mad.
and sometimes
it's for something unreasonable.
and how they're behaving
is irrational.
and asking you to deal with it
is unfair.
but you should appreciate
someone who can be honest
about their feelings,
even if it sounds ridiculous.
because it's better than telling you
they're fine when they're not.

if someone wants to be

a part of your life,

they would be

trying as hard

as you are right now

to be a part of theirs.

if you feel it, say it.

don't evade it. don't disguise it.

sometimes the best way to express yourself,

is to be completely raw.

you deserve to have

what you want

out of a relationship.

EXACTLY what you want.

not a diluted version of it.

loving someone is easy.
but when you're in a relationship
that isn't benefiting you,
loving someone becomes a chore.
you need more joy in your life,
not another job.

your problems may be more severe,
but that doesn't mean someone else's problems
are any less deserving of your time.
remember, what may not be a challenge for you
is still a hardship for someone else.
don't lose your ability to sympathize.

not everyone is as poised
and well-mannered as you.
sometimes you need to let things slide.
pick your battles.

you're not going to like everyone.

not everyone is going to like you.

learn to be okay with it.

if we spent our days

addressing every rumour ever told about us,

we would miss out on a whole lot of life.

the people that know you

already know what is true about you.

forget the rest.

go live.

you shouldn't have to try this hard

when looking for love.

it results in attracting people into your life

who shouldn't be there.

you will find yourself settling for things

you never would've settled for.

there's a plan.

allow it to unfold.

it cannot do so

if you're forcing it in a specific direction.

ever find yourself playing a part for someone?

working hard to show them

that you're the right person for them?

the truth is,

you're not.

and they're not right for you either.

an exaggerated version of you

is still not you.

those who love you

want what's best for you.

and according to them,

what's best

is what *they* know to be true.

don't get mad at them

for wanting the same for you.

remind yourself of this

the next time you're annoyed

by unwanted advice.

your soul is born whole.

and as life progresses

and hardships chip away at you,

pockets begin to form.

believe that God allows for this

to happen on purpose.

because He has made it

so that when true love comes along,

it finds a home in these pockets,

it fills them to the brim,

it makes you whole again.

it's okay to get mad.

the problem arises when we take it too far -

into the realm of spite.

anger is okay

when we use it to be real about our emotions.

it's not okay

when we use it as revenge on others.

if someone puts you down,
you should feel sad –
not for yourself, though -
for them.
what a life they must lead
if their ultimate pleasure
is found in criticizing others.

you shouldn't have to

convince someone to be with you.

don't insult your significant other in front of people.

if you have a problem,

address it privately.

when you openly disrespect the person you love,

you make others think

they have permission to do the same.

forgive, and mean it.

when you don't,

what you're angry about

is free to show up in every disagreement you have.

it becomes the number one tool

you use to hurt the person who has wronged you.

put it to rest.

compromise:

if you don't create space for it,

there will only ever be room

for just you.

a break up

is not where you should end up

after every argument.

learn how to have a fight.

disagreements should not

be a threat to your relationship.

the relationships that make it

have two people

who share a partnership.

how they behave,

and the choices that they make,

they do for the betterment of them as a unit,

not just as two separate entities.

at times, we all need a break from people.

and that's okay.

but when it's no longer about needing space

and just about punishing someone –

stop.

don't lose sight of why you're doing this.

the goal is to improve your relationship,

not sabotage it.

sometimes we keep people we love

out of our lives

because once upon a time

they didn't deserve a spot in it.

and we have this sense of obligation

to stick to our decision

even when they've changed.

don't let this be the only reason you're apart.

love doesn't fade,

it transforms.

what once used to be

like fireworks that were easy to ignite,

now resembles

a calm fire that takes work to stay lit.

but it isn't any less worthwhile in its new form.

and if you don't train yourself to recognize this change,

you will think there's nothing left to fight for.

there is someone out there

who's meant for you.

if you settle for someone

who is sort of what you're looking for,

you will never meet the person

who is everything you're looking for.

if you don't think it's a big deal –

the difference between being "sort of" happy

and being entirely happy

IS a big deal.

we dismiss the attention
when it's given freely.
and then fight for it
when it's taken away.
cherish the person you love
when they're here,
not when they're gone,
and you have to get them back.

some people do wrong unintentionally –

it's called a mistake.

others do wrong intentionally,

call it a mistake

and hide behind it hoping no one notices.

know the difference.

it's okay to give second chances.

there are some who deserve it.

good people make mistakes, too.

friendships should be taken more seriously.
it's easy to find people
who will tell you what you want to hear.
you need friends
who will tell you what you deserve to hear.
and what you deserve isn't always pleasant.
but they would rather you hear the truth.
because they know
that making you a good human being
is better than flattering you for the time being.

you say you want change

in your relationship.

instead of trying to adjust

the person you're with –

adjust yourself.

reach out first,

compromise first,

end an argument first,

apologize first.

if you want change –

be the one to initiate it.

winning is fun, I know.

but not when it comes to your relationship.

the goal isn't to master every argument,

to one-up the other person,

to find their weaknesses

and use it against them.

your significant other isn't an opponent,

and this isn't a competition.

you're on the same team.

being formal is not how
heart-to-heart conversations work.
be candid.
lay your emotions out on the table.
now is not the time for scripts.

beautiful hearts
last longer than
beautiful faces.

sometimes people are afraid
of what they don't understand.
the only way to erase that fear,
is to teach them
that they have nothing to be scared about.
when it comes to our differences,
help unite us, instead of dividing us.

don't put yourself in that situation again,

where you know you're going to leave

as frustrated

as when you left the first time.

end the cycle.

your significant other
should be an extension of you;
a reflection of the person
you have worked hard to become.
they are whom
you're spending a lifetime with,
the person
your future children will be 50% of.

choose wisely.

trying to change you,
and trying to make you a better person
are different things.
don't confuse the two
and refuse the latter.

sometimes,

distance isn't created on purpose.

sometimes,

you just get to a point in life

where you no longer expect things

from certain people.

there's no good reason

not to be with the one you love.

you're both alive, aren't you?

this world is filled with people

who were stripped of a chance.

you have one.

don't waste it.

while you were apart from each other,
accept that they met new people,
and learned new things.
because it all played a role
in helping them realize
that YOU are where they belong.

you can extend a helping hand,
but someone needs to be reaching back.
otherwise it's just you,
pulling them out from a place
they're not ready to leave yet.
sometimes the best way to help someone
is to allow them
to want it for themselves first.

if your significant other's presence in your life

must be filtered

because they don't always fit into it -

you're with the wrong person.

you're not mad at them.

you're mad about something else

and you're taking it out on them.

what's the real problem?

resolve it.

misdirected anger

and the arguments that result from it

are a waste of everyone's time.

when you wake up in the morning,

who do you think of?

where your mind goes

when it's at its clearest,

is where you belong.

when we make a mistake,

sometimes our reaction is to get defensive;

attempt to rationalize what we've done

even when we know we've screwed up.

as if making a mistake

isn't painful enough for the people we love.

we're doing even more harm

by not taking responsibility for it.

if this lifetime

gives you a kind, sincere man,

invest in him.

good hearts and honest words

are hard to find these days.

come home to someone
who softens your heart.
this world can leave it hardened.

if you're in a relationship,

and being around happy couples

makes you bitter –

you're in the wrong relationship.

cheating over and over again

isn't a mistake –

it's a lifestyle.

if only we were

as good at pointing out someone's great qualities

as we are at pointing out their flaws.

when you insult people,

you chip away at their spirit.

we should never be contributors to that.

a good relationship

is one consisting of two people

who found happiness individually.

two happy people aren't pressured

to create happiness for each other.

they're free to intensify

what they already have.

so, you took a risk

and it was unsuccessful.

it's okay.

no, really – IT'S OKAY.

the reason you feel awful

isn't because it didn't work out.

it's because you have people in your life

who will never let you forget that it didn't.

get rid of them.

now, keep going.

settling for the wrong person

is more exhausting

than waiting for the right one.

we're afraid of feelings.

loving too much

means exposing ourselves to vulnerability.

it's easier to numb emotions

to a manageable amount.

so that we can abort at a moment's notice.

this is no way to love.

he's making excuses to you.

and you're making excuses for him.

what a vicious cycle.

you deserve to be with someone
as remarkable as you.
imagine the unbelievable good
that could come of such a union?

they may be okay with being rude.

but you're not them.

and you shouldn't be okay

with transforming into a version of them

just because you must encounter them.

and that means being kind

even when they aren't.

because who they choose to be

shouldn't affect who you have chosen to be.

want to know how you really feel?
watch what happens to you
when you run into them unexpectedly.
or when you know you're going to see them -
and then they walk in.
that's how you really feel.

the point isn't to find a partner

who's going to agree

with every decision you make.

you need someone who can accept

that sometimes you're going to make ones

that they don't like.

people seek revenge

thinking it's the only way

to re-gain control of a situation.

it's not.

in fact, revenge is the complete loss

of control and composure.

this is not the justice you're looking for.

if you've decided
to address the problem,
resolve the problem,
and forgive the problem,
then there's no need
to ever bring it up again.
learn how to navigate through mistakes
so it doesn't interrupt your happiness.

my definition of success

doesn't look like your definition of success.

and that's the point –

it doesn't have to.

we're all contributing to this world

in different ways.

all of it matters.

if you can't show happiness to others

amidst their successes,

that happiness will never reach you.

instead it bounces off this wall you've created,

woven with envy and resentment.

if you want more joy of your own,

give it with sincerity to others.

they may have everything.

you may not.

but for you,

this is enough.

for them,

it will never be enough.

and there's nothing worse than living a life

where you can never be satisfied.

apologies aren't meant to be exhausted,

used again and again

to smooth over the same mistakes.

being a good person

isn't based on your ability to apologize.

it's based on what you choose to do

after the apology.

at the end of the day,

people who don't know the whole story

will make you out to be anything they want.

but half a story

doesn't make it a true story.

it isn't because
you weren't loving hard enough.
it's because
you were loving the wrong person.

we should be spending our precious time

loving the people we love,

not hating the people we hate.

if you decide to keep someone

who did you wrong,

you can't spend the rest of your days

complaining about their behaviour.

remember,

it's the life YOU chose for yourself.

jealousy throws you into a competition
that doesn't even exist.
suddenly, you're going out of your way
to prove that your life is better,
your relationship is better,
the way you look is better.
a more worthwhile way to use your energy
is to invest it into *actually* improving your life.

you shouldn't feel threatened by others.

get rid of the animosity

by recognizing that they're great, too.

it doesn't make you any less great.

who you are is amazing.

don't question it just because

someone else has shown up in the picture.

not every conversation
needs to turn into an argument.
when you're constantly in battle-mode,
you're choosing to walk into wars
that don't even exist.

you don't want to be with people

who don't want to be with you.

let that nonsense go.

it's well below what you deserve.

the truth may hurt.

but withholding it

to save people

from the pain of it

is what's doing the real harm.

there's an entire life out there

waiting to be lived.

stop wasting your days

monitoring someone else's days.

if you're looking for a lifetime partnership,

you're not going to find it

in someone who strokes your ego.

you need someone who isn't afraid

to hurt your feelings,

if it means helping you become a better human.

everything good that you have in this world

you should want others to have, too.

learn to want for more than just yourself.

want for your family,

want for your friends,

want for humanity.

no matter how annoyed

you are at the world today,

there is someone out there

depending on your kindness.

do not let them down.

about the author

after experiencing the healing power of words, Renuka decided to share her snippets of wisdom with everyone through her popular blog. guided by her pen, she embarked on a journey to change lives and help others work through their own moments of darkness. her second book will undoubtedly extend that power to many, many more. she lives in Toronto, Canada, and continues to update her blog at renukawrites.tumblr.com